The 201 Best Things Ever Said!

0 43422 69519 5

Great Quotations Publishing Company, Inc.

Compiled by: Robyn Griggs
Cover Design by: Darren Thompson
Typeset and Design by: Caroline Solarski and
Julie Otlewis

— —

© 1995 Great Quotations Publishing Company, Inc.

Published by Great Quotations Publishing Company, Inc.
1967 Quincy Court
Glendale Heights, Illinois 60139

ISBN: 1-56245-079-4

Printed in Hong Kong

> **"It is a good thing for an uneducated man to read a book of quotations."**
>
> — Winston Churchill

When words fail you, it's always reassuring to know you can turn to someone else's. The famous, the infamous, the little known and the unknown offer the most profound, pithy and powerful words in this marvelous collection of classic quotes from all walks of life. The following phrases are the tip of the iceberg, the cream of the crop among the volumes of quotables available to us.

Who can really say what is "best". Well, this is our "best" guess. Why 201?—That's all we needed to print this book!

Enjoy!

1 ♦ The only way to avoid being miserable is not to have enough leisure to wonder whether you're happy or not.

— George Bernard Shaw

2 ◆ When ideas fail, words come in very handy.

— Goethe

◆◆

3 ◆ Life is just one damned thing after another.

— Elbert Hubbard

4 ◆ In our society, men are afraid they won't be man enough and women are afraid they might be considered only women.

— Theodore Reik

5 ✦ Tomorrow is always the busiest day of the week.

— Jonathan Lazear

◆◆

6 ✦ I'm a study of a man in chaos in search of frenzy.

— Oscar Levant

7 ◆ I know God will not give me anything I can't handle. I just wish He didn't trust me so much.

— Mother Teresa

◆◆

8 ◆ Any idiot can face a crisis — it's this day-to-day living that wears you out.

— Anton Chekhov

9 ✦ Ours is a world where people don't know what they want and are willing to go through hell to get it.

— Don Marquis

◆ ◆

10 ✦ If you keep on saying things are going to be bad, you have a good chance of being a prophet.

— Isaac Bashevis Singer

11 ◆ You live in a deranged age — more deranged than usual, because despite great scientific and technological advances, man has not the faintest idea of who he is or what he is doing.

— Walker Percy

12 ◆ Some of us are becoming the men we wanted to marry.

— Gloria Steinem

◆◆

13 ◆ I love Mickey Mouse more than any woman I've known.

— Walt Disney

14 ✦ If you owe $50, you're a delinquent account. If you owe $50,000 you're a small businessman. If you owe $50 million you're a corporation. If you owe $50 billion, you're the government.

— Lynn Townsend White, Jr.

15 ✦ A celebrity is a person who works hard all his life to become well known, then wears dark glasses to avoid being recognized.

— Fred Allen

16 ◆ There are highly successful businesses in the United States. There are also many highly paid executives. The policy is not to intermingle the two.

— Philip K. Wrigley

17 • Marriage is like a bank account. You put it in, you take it out, and you lose interest.

— Irwin Corey

18 ◆ The first human being
who hurled an insult
instead of a stone was
the founder of civilization.

— Sigmund Freud

19 ◆ In the depths of my heart I can't help being convinced that my dear fellow men, with a few exceptions, are worthless.

— Sigmund Freud

20 ◆ I've got to keep breathing. It'll be my worst business mistake if I don't.

— Sir Nathan Meyer Rothschild

◆ ◆

21 ◆ The world is divided into people who do things — and people who get the credit.

— Dwight Morrow

22 ◆ The higher up you go the more mistakes you're allowed. Right at the top, if you make enough of them, it's considered your style.

— Fred Astaire

23 ◆ To me, a job is an invasion of privacy.

— Danny McGoorty

◆◆

24 ◆ Men for the sake of getting a living forget
to live.

— Margaret Fuller

25 ◆ Appreciation is a wonderful thing:
it makes what is excellent in others
belong to us as well.

— Voltaire

26 ◆ By the time we've made it we've had it.

— Malcolm Forbes

◆◆

27 ◆ That money talks I won't deny. I heard it once, it said goodbye.

— Richard Armour

28 ◆ Mothers are fonder than fathers of
their own children because they are
more certain they are their own.

— Aristotle

29 ◆ There has always been a tenuous connection between the American dream and civilized behavior.

— Lawrence Shames

30 ✦ We all have the strength to endure the
misfortunes of others.

— La Rochefoucauld

◆◆

31 ✦ There are some people that if they don't
know, you can't tell 'em.

— Louis Armstrong

32 ♦ The man who complains about the
way the ball bounces is likely the
one who dropped it.

— Lou Holtz

33 ⬥ I have found that little is good
about human beings. In my
experience, most of them are trash.

— Sigmund Freud

34 ◆ We all can't be heroes because somebody has to sit on the curb and clap as they go by.

— Will Rogers

35 ◆ If you want to sacrifice the admiration of many men for the criticism of one, go ahead, get married.

— Katherine Hepburn

36 ⬥ If you haven't got anything nice to say about anybody, come sit next to me.

— Alice Roosevelt Longworth

◆◆

37 ⬥ A man who comes to me for advice, I find out the kind of advice he wants, and I give it to him.

— Josh Billings

38 ◆ Our self-importance requires that we spend most of our lives offended by someone.

— Carlos Castaneda

39 ◆ Parents were invented to make children happy by giving them something to ignore.

— Ogden Nash

40 ♦ The newest computer can merely compound, at speed, the oldest problem in relations between human beings, and in the end the communicator will be confronted with the old problem, of what to say and how to say it.

— Edward R. Murrow

41 ◆ Lots of folks confuse bad management with destiny.

— Kin Hubbard

◆ ◆

42 ◆ You cannot shake hands with a clenched fist.

— Indira Gandhi

43 ◆ If there's a harder way of doing something, someone will find it.

— Ralph E. Ross

◆◆

44 ◆ Little things affect little minds.

— Benjamin Disraeli

45 ◆ There is no money in poetry, but there is no poetry in money, either.

— Robert Graves

46 ◆ One never notices what has been done; one can only see what remains to be done.

— Marie Curie

47 ♦ It's hard to fight an enemy who has outposts in your head.

— Sally Kempton

48 • It was such a lovely day I thought it was a pity to get up.

— Somerset Maugham

49 ⬧ There is no sweeter
sound than the crumbling
of one's fellow man.

— Groucho Marx

50 ◆ I never forget a face, but in your case I'll make an exception.

— Groucho Marx

◆◆

51 ◆ Anyone who says he can see through women is missing a lot.

— Groucho Marx

52 ◆ At times almost all of us envy the animals. They suffer and die, but do not seem to make a "problem" of it.

— Alan Watts

53 ◆ I once wanted to save the world. Now I just want to leave the room with some dignity.

— Lotus Weinstock

◆ ◆

54 ◆ It is of immense importance to learn to laugh at ourselves.

— Katherine Mansfield

55 ◆ An actor's a guy who, if you ain't talking about him, ain't listening.

— Marlon Brando

56 ◆ We promise according to our hopes, and perform according to our fears.

— Dag Hammarskjold

57 ♦ What if the interests of the self were expanded to . . . a God's eye view of the human scene . . . accepting failure as being as natural an occurrence as success in the stupendous human drama . . . as little cause for worry and concern as having to play the role of a loser in a summer theater performance.

— Huston Smith

58 ✦ Everything great in the world comes from the neurotics. They alone have founded our religions and composed our masterpieces. Never will the world know all it owes to them, nor all they have suffered to enrich us.

— Marcel Proust

59 ◆ The day will happen whether or not you get up.

— John Ciandi

◆ ◆

60 ◆ In three words I can sum up everything I've learned about life. It goes on.

— Robert Frost

61 ◆ I arise in the morning torn between a desire to improve (or save) the world and a desire to enjoy (or savor) the world. This makes it hard to plan for the day.

— E. B. White

62 ♦ For a man to achieve all that is demanded of him he must regard himself as greater than he is.

— Goethe

63 ◆ Losing my virginity was a career move.

— Madonna

◆◆

64 ◆ Life is not a spectacle or a feast; it is a predicament.

— George Santayana

65 ⬩ If I had my life to live over again, I'd be a plumber.

— Albert Einstein

66 ◆ I think and think for months and years. Ninety-nine times, the conclusion is false. The hundredth time I am right.

— Albert Einstein

67 ♦ Learn to say no; it will be of more use to you than to be able to read Latin.

— Charles Hadden Spurgeon

◆◆

68 ♦ It is an ironic habit of human beings to run faster when we have lost our way.

— Rollo May

69 ✦ The happy people are failures because they are on such good terms with themselves that they don't give a damn.

— Agatha Christie

70 ❖ The only man who is really free is one who can turn down an invitation to dinner without giving an excuse.

— Jules Renard

71 ◆ It often happens that I wake at night and begin to think about a serious problem and decide I must tell the Pope about it. Then I wake up completely and remember that I *am* the Pope.

— Pope John XXIII

72 ◆ I drink to make other people more
interesting.

— George Jean Nathan

◆◆

73 ◆ Reality is a crutch for people who can't
cope with drugs.

— Lily Tomlin

74 ✦ If I had my life to live over again, I would have a different father, a different wife and a different religion.

— John F. Kennedy

75 ◆ Whenever things get too unpleasant, I burn the day's newspaper, pull down the curtains, get out the jugs, and put in a civilized evening.

— H. L. Mencken

76 ◆ You must do the thing you think you cannot do.

— Eleanor Roosevelt

◆◆

77 ◆ Almost anything you do will be insignificant, but it is very important that you do it.

— Mohandas Gandhi

78 ◆ Depend on the rabbit's foot if you will, but remember it didn't work for the rabbit!

— R. E. Shay

79 ◆ Some people regard themselves
as perfect, but only because they
demand little of themselves.

— Hermann Hesse

80 ◆ Always do sober what you said you'd do drunk. That will teach you to keep your mouth shut.

— Ernest Hemingway

81 ✦ I like to listen. I have learned a great deal from listening carefully. Most people never listen.

— Ernest Hemingway

82 ♦ If you don't decide which way to play with life, it always plays with you.

— Merle Shain

♦ ♦

83 ♦ There is no life without pain just as there is no art without submitting to chaos.

— Rita Mae Brown

84 ◆ Vitality shows not only in the ability to persist but in the ability to start over.

— F. Scott Fitzgerald

85 ◆ Don't let life discourage you;
everyone who got where he is had
to be where he was.

— R. L. Evans

86 ✦ We judge ourselves by what we feel
capable of doing, while others judge
us by what we have already done.

— Henry Wadsworth Longfellow

87 ♦ There are only two forces that unite
men—fear and interest.

— Napoleon Bonaparte

◆ ◆

88 ♦ We cannot solve life's problems except by
solving them.

— M. Scott Peck

89 ◆ The lust for power is not rooted in strength but in weakness.

— Erich Fromm

90 ✦ We are here and it is now. Further than that all human knowledge is moonshine.

— H. L. Mencken

91 ✦ All changes, even the most longed for, have their melancholy, for what we leave behind us is a part of ourselves; we must die to one life before we can enter into another.

— Anatole France

92 ◆ The human landscape of the New World shows a conquest of nature by an intelligence that does not love it.

— Northrop Frye

93 ◆ When you get there, there is no there there. But there will be a pool.

— David Zucker

◆ ◆

94 ◆ The only normal people are the ones you don't know very well.

— Joe Ancis

95 ❖ It isn't what I do, but how I do it. It isn't what I say, but how I say it. And how I look when I do and say it.

— Mae West

96 ◆ Whenever I'm caught between two evils I take the one I've never tried.

— Mae West

◆◆

97 ◆ It's not the men in my life, but the life in my men.

— Mae West

98 ♦ Sometimes in my dreams there are women. When such dreams happen, immediately I remember: "I am a monk."

— Dalai Lama

99 ◆ I used to do drugs. I got so wrecked one night, I waited for a stop sign to change and it did.

— Steve Krabitz

100 ◆ Unless one says goodbye to what one loves, and unless one travels to completely new territories, one can expect merely a long wearing away of oneself.

— Jean Dubuffet

101 ♦ If at first you don't succeed, you're
running about average.

— Ovid

102 ♦ I love mankind; it's people I can't stand.

— Charles Schultz

103 ◆ The artist who aims at perfection in
everything achieves nothing.

— Eugene Delacroix

104 ◆ "Be yourself!" is about the worst advice you can give to some people.

— Tom Masson

105 ◆ Science may carry us to Mars, but it will leave the earth peopled as ever by the inept.

— Agnes Repplier

106 ✦ Though we travel the world over to find the beautiful, we must carry it with us or we find it not.

— Ralph Waldo Emerson

107 ◆ The trouble with life in the fast lane is that you get to the other end in an awful hurry.

— John Jensen

108 ♦ I don't like a man to be too efficient. He's likely to be not human enough.

— Felix Frankfurter

109 ◆ If you tell the truth
you don't have to
remember anything.

— Mark Twain

110 ◆ One small step for man, one giant leap for mankind.

— Neil Armstrong

◆ ◆

111 ◆ Living with a saint is more grueling than being one.

— Robert Neville

112 ♦ Looking back, my life seems like one long obstacle race, with me as its chief obstacle.

— Jack Paar

113 ◆ **Every day people are straying from the church and going back to God.**

— Lenny Bruce

114 ◆ You can't say civilization doesn't advance . . . in every war they kill you a new way.

— Will Rogers

115 ♦ The only way to keep your health is to eat what you don't want, drink what you don't like, and do things you'd rather not.

— Mark Twain

116 ◆ Fewer things are harder to put up with than the annoyance of a good example.

— Mark Twain

117 ◆ The trick will be to seize the opportunities, avoid the pitfalls, and get back home by 6:00.

— Woody Allen

118 ◆ It is not enough to succeed. Others must fail.

— Gore Vidal

◆◆

119 ◆ Never mistake motion for action.

— Ernest Hemingway

120 ✦ Even if you're on the right track, you'll get run over if you just sit there.

— Will Rogers

121 ◆ Expect the worst and your surprises will always be pleasant ones.

— Louis E. Boone

122 ✦ All the things I like to do are either immoral, illegal or fattening.

— Alexander Woolcott

123 ◆ I'd like to live like a poor man with lots of money.

— Pablo Picasso

124 ◆ I do not seek. I find.

— Pablo Picasso

◆◆

125 ◆ If I like it I say it's mine. If I don't I say it's a fake.

— Pablo Picasso

126 ◆ A fat paunch never breeds fine thoughts.

— St. Jerome

◆◆

127 ◆ Life is God's novel. Let him write it.

— Isaac Bashevis Singer

128 ◆ **The human mind always makes progress, but it is a progress in spirals.**

— Madame de Stael

129 ◆ Clothes make the man. Naked people
have little or no influence on society.

— Mark Twain

130 ♦ Freedom is just another word for nothing
left to lose.

— Janis Joplin

♦♦

131 ♦ What does not destroy me, makes me
strong.

— Friedrich Nietzsche

132 ◆ What the world needs is some "do-give-a-damn" pills.

— William Menninger

133 ♦ Income tax returns are the most imaginative fiction being written today.

— Herman Wouk

134 ◆ Only those who dare to fail greatly
can ever achieve greatly.

— Robert F. Kennedy

135 ◆ Technological progress is like an axe
in the hands of a criminal.

— Albert Einstein

136 ◆ **The man who is swimming against the stream knows the strength of it.**

— Woodrow Wilson

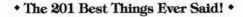
137 ♦ Everything comes to him who
hustles while he waits.

— Thomas A. Edison

138 ♦ People want economy
and they will pay any
price to get it.

— Lee Iacocca

139 ♦ Problems are only opportunities in work
clothes.

— Henry J. Kaiser

◆◆

140 ♦ Everything is so dangerous that nothing is
really frightening.

— Gertrude Stein

141 ◆ Courage is the price that life exacts
for granting peace.

— Amelia Earhart

142 ◆ The last of the human freedoms is
to choose one's attitudes.

— Victor Frankl

143 ◆ Everything has been figured out except how to live.

— Jean-Paul Sartre

144 ♦ Love is an obsessive delusion that is cured by marriage.

— Dr. Karl Bowman

145 ✦ Art washes away from the soul the
dust of everyday life.

— Pablo Picasso

146 ◆ Every human being is a problem in search of a solution.

— Ashley Montagu

147 ◆ Nothing is illegal if a hundred
businessmen decide to do it.

— Andrew Young

148 ♦ I'm an alcoholic. I'm a homosexual. I'm a genius.

— Truman Capote

149 ◆ When I grow up I want to be a little boy.

— Joseph Heller

◆ ◆

150 ◆ There is nothing the body suffers which the soul may not profit by.

— George Meredith

151 ◆ Speak when you're angry, and you'll make the best speech you'll ever regret.

— Lawrence J. Peter

152 ◆ The fiery trials through which we pass will light us down in honour or dishonour to the latest generation.

— Abraham Lincoln

153 ◆ Money can't buy happiness but it will certainly get you a better class of memories.

— Ronald Reagan

154 ♦ The hardest thing to learn in life
is which bridge to cross and which
bridge to burn.

— David Russell

155 ♦ I was born because it was a habit in those days. People didn't know any different.

— Will Rogers

156 ♦ Some American delusions:
   (1) That there is no class-
      consciousness in the country.
   (2) That American coffee is good.
   (3) That Americans are highly sexed
      and that redheads are more
      highly sexed than others.

— W. Somerset Maugham

157 ◆ Outside of a dog, a book is man's best friend. Inside of a dog, it's too dark to read.

— Groucho Marx

◆◆

158 ◆ I never give them hell. I just tell the truth and they think it's hell.

— Harry S. Truman

159 ◆ I'm no Shakespeare, no Hugo, no Balzac. Something a little higher than a louse. That's not overestimating myself, is it?

— Henry Miller

160 ◆ The man with the best job in the country is the vice president. All he has to do is get up every morning and say "How's the President?"

— Will Rogers

161 ♦ God grant me the serenity to accept the things I cannot change, the courage to change the things I can, and the wisdom to know the difference.

— Reinhold Niebuhr

162 ◆ Our greatest glory is not in never
failing but in rising up every time we
fail.

— Ralph Waldo Emerson

163 ◆ Business is like sex. When it's good, it's very, very good; when it's not so good, it's still good.

— George Katona

164 ◆ Imagine there's no country. It isn't hard to do. Nothing to kill or die for. And no religion, too.

— John Lennon

165 ◆ If a man does not keep pace with his companions, perhaps it is because he hears a different drummer. Let him step to the music which he hears, however measured or far away.

— Henry David Thoreau

166 ◆ I came into this world, not chiefly to make this a good place to live in, but to live in it, be it good or bad.

— H. D. Thoreau

167 ◆ In the end, everything is a gag.

— Charlie Chaplin

◆◆

168 ◆ Art is a lie that makes us realize the truth.

— Pablo Picasso

169 ◆ I start every morning with the New York Times. The first thing I do when I get up is read the obituary column. If my name isn't in it, I get dressed.

— Alan King

170 ◆ If was one of those parties where you cough twice before you speak, and then decide not to say it after all.

— P. G. Wodehouse

171 ◆ It is not the truth that makes man great, but man who makes the truth great.

— Confucius

172 ◆ Do not take life too seriously. You will never get out of it alive.

— Elbert Hubbard

173 ♦ **If you aren't fired with enthusiasm, you will be fired with enthusiasm.**

— Vince Lombardi

174 ◆ That's the trouble with "Have a nice day!"— It puts all the pressure on you.

— George Carlin

175 ✦ It has always been a rule never to smoke when asleep, and never refrain when awake.

— Mark Twain

176 ♦ Never put off until tomorrow what you can do the day after tomorrow.

— Mark Twain

177 ♦ The only reason I'm not running for
president is I'm afraid no woman would
come forth and say she slept with me.

— Garry Shandling

◆ ◆

178 ♦ A skeptic is a person who would ask God
for his ID card.

— Edgar A. Shoaf

179 ◆ If there were no bad people, there would be no good lawyers.

— Charles Dickens

180 ✦ Happiness? That's nothing more than health and a poor memory.

— Albert Schweitzer

181 ◆ Illegitimate non-carborundum —
don't let the bastards grind you
down.

— Joseph W. Stilwell -
General, U.S. Army

182 ◆ Great men are meteors designed to
burn so that earth may be lighted.

— Napoleon Bonaparte

183 ♦ Everything is funny as long as it's happening to somebody else.

— Will Rogers

184 ◆ There are some jobs in which it is
impossible for a man to be virtuous.

— Aristotle

185 ◆ Part of the secret of success in life is to eat what you like and let the food fight it out inside.

— Mark Twain

186 ◆ Marriage is one long conversation checkered by disputes.

— Robert Louis Stevenson

187 ◆ The darkest hour of any man's life
is when he sits down to plan how to
get money without earning it.

— Horace Greely

188 ⋆ The great art of life is sensation, to feel that we exist, even in pain.

— Lord Byron

189 ◆ Life is what happens to us while we are making other plans.

— Thomas la Mance

◆ ◆

190 ◆ Only the shallow know themselves.

— Oscar Wilde

191 ◆ In California, everyone goes to a therapist, is a therapist, or is a therapist going to a therapist.

— Truman Capote

192 ◆ Some are born great,
some achieve greatness,
and some have greatness
thrust upon them.

— William Shakespeare

193 ◆ I speak the truth, not so much as I would, but as much as I dare; and I dare a little more, as I grow older.

— Montaigne

194 ◆ When we remember that we are all made, the mysteries disappear and life stands explained.

— Mark Twain

195 ◆ Everyone has a talent. What is rare
is the courage to follow the talent to
the dark places where it leads.

— Erica Jong

196 ◆ How vain it is to sit down to write
when you have not stood up to live.

— Henry David Thoreau

197 ◆ A verbal contract isn't worth the paper it's written on.

— Sam Goldwyn

198 ◆ A woman is the only thing I am afraid of that I know will not hurt me.

— Abraham Lincoln

199 ◆ Make voyages. Attempt them. There's nothing else.

— Tennessee Williams

◆◆

200 ◆ Freedom means choosing your burden.

— Hephzibah Menuhin

201 ◆ When I'm good I'm very good, but when I'm bad I'm better.

— Mae West